The

COMMON
DENOMINATOR

Affirmations and Other Life Lessons

AUDRA Y. MOSES

Charleston, SC
www.PalmettoPublishing.com

The Common Denominator

Paperback ISBN:978-1-64990-420-1

DEDICATION

I would like to dedicate this book to all the strong women I know especially my Mom. Mom, you have been my first inspiration and one of the best people I know. Thank you for being the rock of our family; you should always be put on a pedestal.

TABLE OF CONTENTS

PREFACE

One of my best friends told me, "You should write some of this stuff down". My life has been very eventful. I often thought, "Who would care?" IDK, but I will as I remember. I should have kept a diary. What will I name my book, "Random thoughts", "The common-denominator", "No filter tales", "My life", or just maybe, "IDK", LOL. I'll write my story as if its fiction; change names In order to protect people "involved", but you know who you are! I will put some of these stories on paper, so that others can read some of this bullshit and laugh, cry, or relate.

ACKNOWLEDGEMENTS

I listened to you, Jay Gaines. I asked myself, "What do you have in you that you haven't tapped into?" Everyone has that something. At first my answer was, "nothing". I said to myself, "What a loser I am". Wow, if I think that of myself, what do others think?

I couldn't think of a single thing. Until one day I asked myself that question again and I started writing, typing rather, same thing. Before, I knew it. I wrote 7 pages. I enjoyed it, hope you will.

1

'THE COMMON-DENOMINATOR'

This is my story from 2012-2019. Had I followed my own advice, I would not have made my third mistake. Ready....

So I tapped into my inner most thoughts and this is what happened...

I changed the names of my characters in this story in order to "protect" them; but, if you are reading this, you definitely know who you are.

Terry was who he said he was. "A bad N!$%a". I thought to myself, "Here we go again, Armenta. You are the common denominator. Husband number three (3), Terry.

I asked myself, "You have been married for the third time. What part do you play in this STORY?" Well since, January 25, 2019 I have had time to think about this question. That was the day Terry left. HE sought to prove to me that he was "A bad N!$%a".

* * *

Lesson: Learn from your own life lessons/mistakes before you make them AGAIN. Always keep your eyes open. If it quacks like a duck, it is a duck.

Let me tell our story so that "our" story, tells the story of Armenta & Terry. As I'm typing, I'm thinking, I divorced my second husband for cheating on me, my first husband because we cheated on each other (that wasn't the only reason; we fell out of "love" for each other, we were too young and stupid when we got married but that is another story).; Met my third husband because I helped him cheat on his wife, even though it wasn't the first time for him. I remember I heard his wife say (in a loud and angry voice) over the phone "Another woman, Terry?" That should have been red flags for me; but I chose to "hang in there", I did love this man. I believed the myths he told me about his first wife; stupid, naive me. He told me he loved me after only three months of knowing me (WHAT! red flag). He was horrible with money; that is why he was in debt for over 85 thousand dollars. Most of the debt had to do with the fact that he didn't file his taxes in over 5 years, hospital bills, car repossessions (3 that I know of) , evictions etc... Did I miss something? If that's not a red flag, I don't know what is. Terry was in serious health trouble at one time. He had Sepsis, which is a life threatening condition that arises when the body's response to infection causes injury to its own tissues and organs. He could have died. But by God's grace, Terry got better. I loved Terry. In some ways he was a loving, caring man. He's not all bad, but bad enough for me. Like most of us, he should have been on somebody's couch (psychiatric care) for his issues stemming from his childhood experiences. I told him so; he looked at me as if he saw a ghost. I guess truth slapped him in the face.

He thought that I was pining away for my ex-boy-friend, Sean. But in all actuality, he was pinning away for his ex-girlfriend. I do not think about Sean until he brings him up. If Sean knew this, it would really puff his chest out.

Before Terry got sick, I took a trip to NY, hooked up with Sean, had a wonderful time, and then LIED about it. In hindsight, I should have told the truth. I was afraid. Terry was sick and I almost felt like I caused him to be sick. Until, he chose to place a bugging device on my cell phone, listened and taped conversations that I had with my sister-cousins, Yvette & LaVonne. He heard me tell them about my trip to NY hook up with Sean, and I told them that Terry's penis is like a limp noodle. Unbeknownst to me, Terry would be listening in on a private conversation I was having with my sister-cousins. I heard my grandmother say in my head, "If you go look-ing for something, you just might find it". You did Terry! Mission accomplished! You caught Armenta in a lie; but what did you do, you married her anyway five years later. I thought all was forgiven. I forgave you for spying on me; you forgave me for Sean; so I thought. But, Terry did Not.

❋ ❋ ❋

Lesson: Don't tell your current partner about your past relationship(s). It is none of their business and they may throw it up in your face to prove "a point". Do NOT play "Bob/Betty the Builder" with your relationships. I got that little tad-bit from Malcolm "MJ" Harris. Love you, Malcolm!

2

2012

I sold my 1st home, contingent upon buying my current home. All worked out. Terry and I moved in together. About, three months into our "new" home life, letters from the IRS started flooding in (five letters a day). That's when I found out how much debt Terry was actually in. I told Terry "You have to get an attorney and file bankruptcy. I got him an attorney (I paid for it, Terry didn't have any money, IRA<401K<Savings Nada. By this time we commingled our funds together. Being good with money was one of my strengths. Terry didn't have a problem with it. He knew it would be in his best interest, and it was. We went on trips and our bills were paid on time every time. Good Feeling. I was working for BofA at the moment, he, at a car dealership. I made more money. At first I didn't think that mattered to Terry, but it did. It didn't matter to me; I thought that was the reality at the moment and things would change. His IRS

debt was paid off to the trustee in October 2018. Terry was elated! He started seeing his credit score go up. I made sure his current credit was in EXCELLENT standing. Things were looking good for Terry. When I think about it, Terry was very selfish. Sometimes I wish I could converse with his first wife and get her side of their story. I can only imagine the things she'll say. I've heard his side. I wonder how much is true. You know what they say, "there's his side, her side, and the truth". This is my truth. I will not sugar coat it. I do have MY faults and I know them. My biggest fault is I don't have a filter. I've been told this many times. I'm working on it. If I were to think about it, I'd say I do have a filter. There are thoughts that run through my mind that I do not let come out of my mouth. If you could only read my mind sometimes, the things you will find out.

As I have my alone time, I remember Terry saying to me, I think I'm better than anyone else. I thought, "Really dude, I grew up in the projects do you know how stupid that sounds"? I do like nice things, but who doesn't? N!$%a, please. I know you like nice things. You are a "dry bragger". You brag about things, on the down-low. Your cousin once called you "Big nut swinging, Terry"; you posted your new car (2013 F Sport Lexus) on FB (Facebook) with the caption, "It's not a Porsche, but it will do". Who does that? A dry-bragger, that's who; I bought that car for Terry; he had everyone else thinking it was him. Those close to Terry knew the real deal.

* * *

Lesson: Do not buy into things that
people say about you. It is probably,
how they really feel about themselves.

3

2013

I had to have neck surgery. I had a horrible pain in my neck, after many injections, I decided to have surgery. It was so painful. I was still in contact with Sean and I told him of the surgery. Terry found out (don't know how for sure.humm). I viewed Sean as a good friend. Terry told me I had to cut off communication with Sean. I told Terry he has no right to tell me who I can and cannot speak to. I thought about it and asked myself, "Would You like it, if that was done to you?" My answer "NO"

I cut all communication with Sean off. Terry didn't believe that.

✳ ✳ ✳

Lesson: Do not cut off your friends because of someone else's insecurities.

4

2014-2015

We got married July 24, 2014. My son, Elijah was about 15 yrs. old. He started showing his ass. Mind you Terry came into Elijah's life when he was 8. I met Terry in March 2007, Elijah met him September 2007. At first, they liked each other, I thought. In hindsight, I change his whole dynamic when I married Terry. After we married, Terry and Elijah became jealous of each other. I said that to Terry and he threw a temper tantrum and broke his C-Pap machine by slinging it across the room. I guess he thought that would intimidate me. I was thinking, "This N!$%a is crazy." You're going to break your life-giving machine because you mad and the truth hurts? I blame a large part of their relationship on Ronald, Elijah's dad (husband no. 2). Ronald was a true to life "deadbeat" for a father. He was not a major part of Elijah's life during adolescence.

Elijah had underlying issues with that relationship. But Terry didn't have compassion and understanding of where the bad behavior was coming from, he too lashed out. Now guess who is in the middle, Me. I love my husband and I love my son. But there is never a choice for me. My son would have won that battle. Terry said horrible things about my son's father to him. My belief is, that is a child, and you're the adult. Sometimes it doesn't matter how old you are. Ignorance is bliss and doesn't have an age. That's another reason how I know that Terry was jealous of Elijah. FYI: Terry was 63 years old at the time. How childish was he?

* * *

Lesson: Hold up, Girl. Follow your instincts and gut feelings.

5

2016

This was the year I turned 50. I remember feeling excited; so I decided to throw myself a birthday party. It would be my first and only birthday party I ever had. Some family members and one my best friends' came to town to celebrate with me. Little did I know this was the year Terry started showing his true self.

✤ ✤ ✤

Lesson: Mya Angelou said, "When a person shows you who they are, believe them the first time".

6

2016-2017

I was over it with Elijah threatening living with his dad. I reluctantly challenged him on it; hoping this was just a "growing pain" on Elijah's part. Unfortunately it wasn't; off he goes to his dad's house (the challenge didn't work very well for me). His dad was married at the time. They had two children together and she had a child from a previous relationship. I really liked Ronald's wife and often hoped he had changed and would be good to her. Wrong! He fucked that up too! Elijah got another feel of what his dad was really about. He ended up at my mother's house because he needed to finish out his senior year in HS. My mother's house was in the same school district/zone as Elijah's High School. Elijah had aspirations of joining the Navy. After graduation, Elijah went back to Ronald's house, came back to my house in October before shipping out in November to pursue his dream. All the while, Ronald takes me to court to stop his child support (child support that he did not pay). N!$%a's and flies. The more I deal with N!$%a's, the more I like flies. He lost (or Elijah lost), but I made a discovery; Terry was addicted to porn. My home office window faces our front porch. Terry goes out on the front porch every morning and drinks his coffee. He also takes this time to look at porn on his cell phone. I never said anything to him about it. I just figured that was one of his vices and it didn't deserve mentioning; until one day I had to call him on it. I also discovered, Terry was cheating **on** me with the same woman he cheated **with** on his first wife.

* * *

Lesson: A leopard doesn't change his spots. "Cheating" comes in all different fascists.

7

JANUARY 2018

Terry's son, Terry Jr. and wife, Shirley, came to live with us. Wow, nothing was ever said to me, but I didn't mind. In my mind, it was only for maybe 90 days to help them get on their feet. I don't have a problem helping folks out in their time of need. During this time, I wanted to let my Real Estate License work into a business for myself. I pitched the idea to Terry and he thought it was a good idea. I quit my corporate job and went into business for myself, May 2018. Terry included me on his health insurance immediately because of my departure from corporate America and their employee Health Insurance.

That 90 days of adult children living free turned into 182 days and here comes, Mitch. Terry's other son. His girlfriend kicked him out of their apartment. Excuse me, her apartment unless you recognize Mitch's tenancy as being a squatter, which is what he was. His girlfriend stated Mitch did not financially contribute to bills, he says, he did but guess who had to go. Still, no word from Terry.

August 2018 I had a conversation with Shirley, Terry Jr., and Mitch about them needing each other. I was getting tired of these grown ass adults living freely in my home. Terry didn't want me to have this conversation. Why, I do not know. I told Terry to get them together, in my presence, to organize a plan to leave. I wanted to put a 30 day time frame on it. Terry did not want to give them a time frame. I wonder why. I said alright, but I still had one in mind. They got one, YEAH! They were to move out November 4, 2018. In the meantime, Terry's cousin Samantha (Sam) decides to visit. Mind you, she knows of these grown ass adults living in my home. I guess she does not care. I usually enjoy Sam's company, but this clearly was not the time to visit. She came anyway. I was becoming increasingly agitated by not having my house back. After all, all my kids are grown and living their adult lives on their own. Terry can't say the same for all his kids.

I remember an incident when his family was visiting and was talking on the porch. I was in the living room doing my Yoga in attempt to meditate and calm my spirit. I have a storm door that slams shut when entering and exiting the front porch. Terry and some of his family members were chit-chatting on the porch. I got up from my yoga exercising and asked them not to let the door slam. Sam says "alright baby". I thought that was the end; then I heard Terry say, "This is my mother fucking door, I bought it." I saw RED. I went outside and said, "YOU ain't buy shit" and went back into the house. He comes in the house, no more bragging or boasting and says, "Are you alright? Are you sick?" I said No, but I heard what you said. It was almost as if he was taking all the credit for our living situation, as if HE did all this himself. Dude, don't act like you forgot. None of this "good living" would be possible if it weren't for me. I blame myself for his attitude. I let it go on for so long. I wanted him to feel pride in our home, not bragalicious. My truth: I thank my heavenly father every day for ANY and ALL blessings that were bestowed upon me. I treated Terry like the king of our castle, but don't get it twisted, I am the QUEEN. He didn't treat me as such. He should have. I always said "happy wife, happy life". The wife was not happy. Another incident happened that brings my non-filter mouth into play. Terry's family and I were having a conversation about Terry's step-grandmother's house and I said, "if anything happens to Grandma, her kids would get her house; not bastard children that her husband had before Grandpa married Grandma." That was a very poor choice of words on my part. I made a statement and used the word "bastard" not thinking I was stepping on toes or hurting feelings. I say things without thinking, but I NEVER mean to hurt anyone's feelings. This is one of my faults I'm working on. Pray for me. If I offended anyone then he or she should have come to me. I did not think I did.

The next day I was having my morning cup of coffee, as I usually do, when Sam walks in the kitchen and throws a half empty Mountain Dew bottle in my garbage. She looked me directly in my eye in an antagonizing way. Everyone knows I am anal when it comes to recycling. I said, "Sam, that bottle belongs in the recycling bin". She commences to tell me that she is not going to get that bottle out of the garbage can. If you want something done, you have to do it yourself. It's not dirty because I just emptied the trash. I got the bottle out of the trash can and I said, "How are you going to tell me what the fuck you ain't gonna do in MY mother fuckin house?". An argument ensues. Terry comes in the room and says, "I don't want to hear you guys fussing, I ain't got time for this". I couldn't believe what I was hearing. I couldn't believe he didn't come to my defense. I am the wife and this is MY HOUSE! This could have been rectified by simply saying to Sam, "This is my wife's home, you need to respect her wishes, if she wants you to recycle, do IT! End of story." But he didn't. He scolded the both of us as if we were children. I told Terry to come to our bedroom; I need to talk to him. I simply said (through soak filled crying eyes), "How would you feel if someone came into your home and told you what they ain't gonna do in your home?" He said he wouldn't like it. He then got up, went into the living room and told everybody they had to leave (GTFO). I was shocked and said, "Everyone's going to think I told you to tell them to get out". Terry said, "I don't give a fuck". I guess HE was sick of those grown ass adults living in our home as well. They only had three days to go before their apartment was ready; three days to fend for themselves. Put your grown panties on and take care of yourself (grown ass adult children).

I stayed in my bedroom crying as I watched them march out the door through my security camera. I heard Sam say "We have to stop at a laundry-mat and do laundry". I thought, "Not at my house, bitch. See what you did? LOL

Terry took their leaving hard and broke down crying. I often wondered why. He's the one that kicked them out of the house. My cousin seems to think that Terry felt emasculated his' jig is up' she said. He caused this mess; maybe that's why He was so upset. He felt Guilty.

Before all this transpired, we found a house to renovate. The house came into play because Terry mentioned our business to a co-worker of his (dry-bragging). Terry's bragging came in handy that time. His co-worker said his aunt was looking to sell her home. It was empty; she had a stroke, and couldn't care for the home any longer. Terry told me about it, and I said let's look into it. Hence, our first home renovation after two other failed attempts and money lost. It took about 6 months to finish; which should only have taken 2-3 months.

Time passes and Terry says to me, "You seem happier now than you were before the grown adult children came to live with us. I said, "That ought to tell you something". Our marriage was declining rapidly. Terry was very bitter about having to kick his grow adult children out the house and took his anger out on Armenta. Armenta suggested getting marriage counseling. Terry got so agitated with Armenta, he wrote a resignation let-ter from the business that was created and the only thing he was seeking from the company was $7000.00. This was the amount he took out his 401K to put into the com-pany. Armenta took out a total of $50,000.00 from her IRA. She told him in a letter that she wrote that she will re-visit his resignation later because "feelings" were high.

I recall an incident when Terry approached Armenta for sex and Armenta wasn't in the mood. Granted, Armenta is always never in the mood but he made such a scene; Armenta told him she wasn't one of those twen-ty or thirty year olds that he watches everyday fucking (porn). He looked at her as if he saw a ghost. Armenta said, "Yeah, I know you watch porn every day; but if you want to impress me show me some fifty-sixty year olds fucking". She never saw him watching porn again; or, he made sure he didn't allow himself to get caught again. There was another incident where he told Armenta that Apple sent an update to his phone and all his apps were deleted. Armenta thought to herself, "He must think I'm a fool." It was clearly something on that phone he didn't want me to see. I wonder what it was. Porn flicks, conver-sations with another woman, maybe?

The marriage was increasingly declining. Armenta said to Terry, "We need counseling". They got counsel-ing. There was only three sessions of counseling. First session with the couple, Armenta and Terry; second, one-on-one with each; third, came the psychologists recommendation for the couple. She suggested that we need time apart to see if that may or may not bring us back together. I said I was not leaving my house and I asked Terry if he would be willing to leave. He said yes and left, January 25, 2019. I think Terry left the home with the intent on returning. However, while he was gone, Armenta discovered some very disturbing things.

Armenta got the house sold and closed March 2019. Social media isn't very good for couples; especially, when you have an "immature" partner that posts their business on social media. I always lived with the mantra "Say it, forget it, write it, regret it." I guess I'm writing it down now, LOL. But I don't regret anything I'm writing because it's my truth. In fact, social media has broken up many relationships. Mine included. It tells the truth of how someone really feels if you listen carefully and read posts. Terry was on Facebook since 2015 or sooner, IDK (I don't know). I, on the other hand, was not on social media until I started my business in 2017. Since then, I've been using FB for business only. I thought it would help with my business, and it did. It also revealed some truths about Terry. Terry has posted a picture of his ex-girlfriend, sitting on his lap on his page. Rhoda. The picture was about thirty years old, the caption read, "Rhoda! A little something for a bad day! Flowers bring joy!! Love Terry." At first, I thought nothing of it, until … I looked deeper. Terry had been posting sweet nothings to Rhoda on her Facebook page since 2016. One caption read, "Ageless! As beautiful as you were the first time our eyes met. What's the secret?" then he posted a kissing emoji that said WOW! I was flabbergasted! I brought this to Terry's attention and he acted like he was clueless. Yeah right N!$%A! This is a woman that you cheated on your first wife with. Little did I know this was happening again I then went to Rhoda's page where I discovered this behavior has been going on for quite some time (since 2016 maybe sooner, IDK). She found out about me because I pressed 'like' on a picture she posted of her and her husband, and she then blocked me from her page (I wonder how?...hmm), but not before I got an eye full of Terry's mess. The wife is always the last to know. Plus, I'm not one to look at what people were doing on social media. I never thought for the life of me Terry would be that person to air his dirty laundry on social media, like he's Kanye West or something. Damn, I mean he is 65 years old. You're too old to be playing reindeer games. When he posted the picture of them two on his page, his son Mitch commented on it. Terry said to him, "This is the one that got away" WOW, slap me in the face again. I never thought I was "pretty", but I did think I was "easy on the eye". But, when your husband is telling another woman how Ageless. Stunning, Beautiful, Pretty, Awesome, A killer smile; you start questioning your own looks.

I showed my family all his inappropriate comments to Rhoda. I told Terry I wanted him to take them all down. He refused. WOW, Slap! That told me something too. He was baiting this woman in hopes of her biting his bait again. My cousin seems to think Rhoda isn't thinking about Terry. She's "happily" married. I don't know this to be true but I do know that Terry is not. He also posted a comment on a picture of her and her sister, "Two of the prettiest women I know". Really, N!$%A? I also discovered some things he posted about me. Things like he's been loyal and he couldn't trust me. All I could do is read these things with my mouth hanging open. If anyone has been loyal, it's me boo, not YOU!

He tried to reconcile, he said to me, "Didn't I always tell you, you were the prettiest woman in the room? Yeah, N!$%A I guess I am until these two other mother-fuckers walk in. Tell that to someone else who will believe your bullshit! I *know when a player is trying to play. I wasn't born yesterday. So, Yes, you ARE* ***"THAT N!$%A"***

BITCH N!$%a N!$%a N!$%a N!$%a N!$%a BITCH N!$%a N!$%a N!$%a

You're just giving me more shit to write about. So... Terry finds out that he still has a joint account that he was not taken off of with Armenta. This is a "keep the change account" that is linked to Armenta's checking account. Terry is not associated WITH and does NOT have access to the checking account. He doesn't contribute to this account what-so-ever. Armenta solely has since Terry left. He sees that he still has access to this account, sends a Zell transfer of $500 to his son with a note to his son "Don't spend this money". NOW this mother fucker is stealing from me! What a snake in the grass! My family seems to think that Terry is in need of some money, that's why he stole my money.

All I can say is you have really changed my opinion of you. I thought you were a good guy with some issues. Now you are just a fucked-up individual. How can you look yourself in the mirror and be proud of what you see? I almost want to text your son and tell him what you did. I don't because that's your son and I like Nigel. He shouldn't be put in the middle of this shit even though you put him there. He may be wondering and asked Terry the question. I'm sure you lied to him. Children tend to love their parents unconditionally. I often wonder what kids think about their parents when their parents are fuckup individuals. I guess they love them through their flaws.

I have come to terms with knowing that you are not going to give me my money back. Wait, there's more. Terry gets a tattoo the next day; a tattoo that clearly costs about $500.

BITCH N!$%a N!$%a N!$%a N!$%a N!$%a BITCH N!$%a N!$%a N!$%a

Ok, now you are suing me for half of the proceeds on the fix & Flip property? Are you serious? That property was not the cash cow; YOU seem to think it was. I spent 50K out of my IRA to this date to your measly 7K from your 401K. N!$%a, please. Now you want HALF THE PROCEEDS from this flip that you may have put 5% of your time into to my 95%. Where are you getting the money from to sue me? I wonder. Terry ends up with Rhoda. Good luck, girl! Terry and Armenta divorce. The End.

* * *

Lesson: Never marry a BITCH N!$%a.
Never trust a BITCH N!$%a. Know a
BITCH N!$%a when you see one!

8

AFFIRMATIONS

I was sitting here listening to "It ain't over", by Maurette Brown Clark. I like some Gospel music. I grew up in the Jehovah Witness faith. It is my foundation religion if that makes any sense. Growing up, I have had affiliation with many other religions including, 7th Day Adventist, Baptist, Catholicism, Buddhism, Judaism, Muslim, Israelites, and Fiver Percenters. There are so many religions on this earth. Jehovah says it will be many in the bible, but there's only ONE true God. Getting knowledge of these other religions and what their beliefs are, I always come back to my roots. In life you have to find your higher power. It is my hearts belief that there is a higher power greater than human. Man could not accomplish the true miracles that are in front of us. If you just look up at the sky and see all the beauty amongst the stars and clouds; how can a mere mortal do this? I believe Jehovah is the one and only true God and Jesus is his son. Jehovah gave us his only begotten son as a ransom sacrifice for our sins. When I think about the concept, I don't fully understand Jehovah's reasoning behind it but who am I to question the most high, my creator. That's my heavenly father and I trust him no matter what. As I write this I'm sobbing like a baby trying to imagine having to see hateful people kill my son. Knowing that almighty, Jehovah, can bring him back to life; it is still no consolation of seeing hateful humans, who are beneath Gods son, kill him. WOW, that's powerful.

I know Jehovah has my back. He has proven that to me time and time again; even though I do truly not deserve his grace. I've done some stupid things in my life and it's amazing to me that it took me 53 years to be in a position to receive God, listen, and learn. I am realizing that everyone is put on earth for a reason. Writing my story may be my reason. Sharing my story may help someone else or not. I don't know what this epiphany of mine will bring but the journey is fulfilling and writing makes me feel good.

As I listen to Lionel Richie "Zoom"; I realize he's living his "purpose". I need to live mine; writing may be it. It sure calms my spirit.

* * *

Lesson: Live your true purpose in life whatever that may be!

9

MS (MULTIPLE-SCLEROSIS)

I have relapsing-remitting MS (Multiple-Sclerosis). I was diagnosed in 2006. I stayed in denial of my disease for a long time. I wondered, "How the hell did I get this disease. I'm a black woman! This is not a black woman's disease. Wrong! It's an "anybody's" disease. I combat my disease with Yoga, positive thoughts, good friends and family, and homeopathic remedies. The trigger for this disease is STRESS. I try not to be stressed; but life happens and life can be stressful. You have to be your own advocate and know what is good for YOU and what is not. If it is not good, let it go.

Time alone gives me the opportunity to think about things that went on more clearly. It's a humbling reality. Sometimes I get lonely. Other times I'm glad to be alone! I can talk to myself out loud and nobody will care. I never lived alone, until now. It's always been, me my parents and brothers>me and a husband,>me a husband and kids> me and kids> never me alone until now. I am getting to know ME and enjoy my own company. I do know that I will NOT marry again. Marriage and I DO NOT get along. I AM the Common Denominator of failed marriages. I'm working on my faults. I will not be good for anyone else until about 2022+. So, if you ever hear me with someone before that time or marriage, that's a damn lie! I'm trying to learn me and love me!

Oh, by the way, don't think I don't know YOU (you know who you are) tampered with my hot water heater before you left and turned the pilot light off so that I wouldn't have hot water. I know what YOU did! Everything you do in the dark always comes to light.

※ ※ ※

Lesson: Trust your gut. Don't jump into anything in life without thoroughly examining first. Always do your research! Try to live your life stress free.

10

P-GOD

P God was a Five Percenter. Five Percenters' were a religious group that believed they were the 5 percent of the nation that knew the truth. As a kid my friends and I thought five percenters were a bunch of knuckleheads that didn't know the truth if it hit them upside the head. My girlfriends' and I were the same girls that attended Elementary and Junior H.S. with them. We knew them as Robert, Chris, Rodney, Paul, and Richard. We get to High School and now they were to be referred to as: Rakim Allah, Everlasting, Shah-Kim, Supreme, and the list goes on. They referred to themselves as "gods" and the women as "earths". That was the stupidest shit I heard in my life. I don't normally like to say disparaging things about any religion, but in this case the shoe fits. As we got older that religion was no longer practiced by the guys. Although some still embraced some of the concepts like, no eating pork, no drugs, renaming themselves, and still refer to themselves as, "god". To me and what I believe, Five Percenters' are not TRUTHFUL. There is no way in hell I'm going to believe any of these idiots; I knew since 2nd grade, convince me they are "gods". I read up on this religion of the five percenters'; I encourage people to do the same thing. There are two topics I try to stay away from engaging in conversation and they are Religion and Politics. These two subjects always end up in debates if you're not on the same team.

Back to P-God; I believe he liked me romantically, but the feeling was not mutual. Maybe the feeling could have grown but P-God was a drug-dealer. I did not gravitate toward drug-dealers. To me, it was a short lived "profession" and drug-dealers were bad news. I didn't know he was a drug-dealer at first; it was soon revealed to me later. P-God was from uptown; Harlem to be exact. One thing I do know is that you can't go into someone else's hood and sell your drugs on their turf. One day P-God came to visit me. He whistled outside my second floor bedroom window to come downstairs. We were sitting on the bench in front of my building talking; our backs were facing the street when all of a sudden three guys from the neighborhood yoked P-God, ripped his pockets and stole his drugs and money. We didn't see them coming. One of the guys looked at me and told me to take my ass back upstairs. I did just that; I was scared. P-God ran off toward the subway station, crying and humiliated. I watched from the window in the building as P-God ran toward the No. 2 train. I didn't hear from

P-God for two weeks when all of a sudden he whistled for me to come downstairs at my bedroom window. I lived on the second floor in a three story building. I came downstairs; we talked in my building on the second floor landing. P-God had a gun. He vowed to avenge his aggressors. He didn't stay long. I guess he was being more careful this time. Little did I know it would be the last time I saw P-God.

About a month pasted and I heard that one of the guys that robbed P-God was shot, one killed, and the other is missing. One guy that was shot wears a colposcopy bag.

I don't know what happened to P-God. He could be dead, in jail, or still hiding. He could be very successful. IDK, but I hope the latter is true. Hell, I don't know his government name (real name).

※ ※ ※

Lesson: Fast money is not always Good money. Know the people you want to do "business" with it may mean life or death.

11

LOSS

The first time I experienced loss, I was 10 yrs. Old. I was in the fifth grade. My teachers' name was Mrs. Keilson. I went to P.S. 251 in the Canarsie section of Brooklyn. My public school was predominately of the Caucasian persuasion. I give those details so that you can imagine yourself coming from a predominately Black and Hispanic neighborhood into a different daytime demographic. Actually, when I think about it, I didn't dwell on my environment until racism beard its ugly face to me in Junior H.S.

I was six years old when my mom "busted" us (myself and my older brother) out of the zoned school we were in for a better education. My mom said she wanted us to know how to get along with white folks because she knew we would need to know that in life.

"Busing" was popular then. It allowed kids in the "hood" to attend schools in other neighborhoods; "white" neighborhoods to be exact. Unfortunately, schools in the predominately Caucasian neighborhoods got better education than those in Black neighborhoods. Shame, isn't it? That's the world we live in.

Kim Gardner was my best friend. Kim was also black, but she lived in Canarsie. She lived in a more up-scaled project, in my opinion. There were no pissy elevators, no drug addicts nodding in the hallways, or pimps and prostitutes. The pimps and prostitutes were no big deal since they were my neighbors anyway. The hallways in the "white" neighborhoods always stayed clean and no pissy elevators detected. Believe it or not white folks do get better section eight housing; even in poverty and lower income neighborhoods black folks are still discriminated against.

Back to Kim; to me, she was beautiful. We played together and liked the same things, even boys. I remember a boy in the next grade up named Robert. I didn't care much for Robert. I liked his older brother Kenny. Kim liked Robert. Robert liked me. In my young mind, I wondered why the older brother wasn't more appealing to Kim as he was to me. I guess I always like "older" men. I believe I had "daddy issues". Excuse me, have.

Spring break came and Kim and her family went to Disney World. At the time, I didn't know anything about Disney World except it was a fun place for kids. I had no aspirations about going but Kim did. She was excited. I didn't see the big deal. Disney World was never a staple for kids in my circle. I guess exposure or thinking "we" could not possibly get to go to Disney World was not an option so we didn't dwell on it. Kim and her family drove and on the way back Kim and her brother, Kenyatta, was killed in an automobile accident. I believe her parents survived. Kim and her brother were in the back seat. I didn't hear the news until I got back to school when spring break was over. Other kids came up to me and told me Kim died, in a nonchalant way. I didn't believe it and I told them they were lying; but they weren't. My heart was crushed. I can't imagine how their mother must have felt losing two of her children at one time. I remember there being a moment of silence in school. I lost it. I'm 53 years old now and it still saddens me to think about it 43 years later.

* * *

LESSON: Loss is inevitable. Death is inevitable. Love people while they are still here.

12

REDEMPTION

Here comes Jackie Lewis, my nemesis. She was a grade older than I and a lot bigger. I was always very petite. She tormented me every chance she got. When I think back, there had to be some jealously involved. I was a cute little girl if I do say so myself; Jackie not so much. She would try to pick fights with me but I was scared. In my 10 year old mind, I had to fight her back in an effort to stop her from antagonizing me. One day we were in the school cafeteria and she hit me. I hit her back and this went on for several minutes until a teacher saw us and broke up the "fight". I was so relieved and felt like I was saved from an ass whipping. Fortunately, we were at the end of the school year and I would not have to deal with Jackie. I managed to avoid her, the remainder of the school year. She was leaving P.S. 251 and going to Junior

H.S. Roy H. Mann. I was dancing and cheering. I would not have to deal with Jackie Lewis for a year.

It was my turn to go to Junior H.S. I was 12 years old. My posse grew bigger. Janice, Tressy, and Tawana were my friends in the neighborhood that were "bused out" as well. We all rode the subway train and bus together to school. Janice, Tressy, and Tawana went to Roy H. Mann a year ahead of me because their elementary school didn't have a sixth grade, mine did. Little did I know Jackie was tormenting them in Junior H.S. (smh) Jackie was a bully. She only picked on those who were smaller than she. Janice was the same size as Jackie so she was not picked on. In my mind Jackie was no longer a threat; Jackie didn't see it that way. The torment resumed. I thought to myself in order to get Jackie off my back once and for all, I have to fight this motherfucka. We were scheduled to fight on the city bus after school. I had some people on my side now; of course I couldn't go out like no punk. I was still scared but felt more confident. I remember being on the bus ready to fight when all of a sudden, Janice jumped in front of me, whipped Jackie's ass and when she finished Tressy started to do the same thing. The city bus stopped in front of South Shore H.S. and they kicked Jackie off the bus, crying. I was in disbelief. Janice said, "She had no business picking on people smaller than her". It seems that Jackie was notorious for this behavior. Her reign was over. She never bothered me or my people again. In fact, I never saw her again, go figure. Mabey her mother took her out of the school thinking she was the one being bullied. Back to the hood she went. Moving forward, she's gone; I was happy.

Here comes Ronald. Little did I know this would be husband number two? He was cute, his kissing skills, not so much.

�֍ ֍ ֍

Lesson: STOP bullying people; it will back-fire on you sooner or later.

13

HYPERTENSION

I came across this story and wanted to include it. I often think why things happen. I cannot allow someone to abuse me on purpose. Pain does not last forever. There comes a time when you have to put on your big girl panties and go through life no matter how much it hurts.

I had a text war with my brother. He has high blood pressure and refuses to acknowledge or take medication for it. I told him of a supplement I was taking for my MS. I was only telling him because of the "proven" results from it. Why did I do that? He took my telling him this fact the wrong way. He started getting offended and loud. He thinks he can cure his high blood pressure with herbs, leaves, and roots. He concocted this mixture and put it in some water with chlorophyll. He believes this is a gift from God. He actually believes he has the cure for most ailments, including cancer. NI$%a are you crazy? I think you are. I told him, "Don't you know high blood pressure is the "silent killer"; haven't you been warned not once, not twice, but more than three times? Now, every time I ask him about his blood pressure he gives me some bullshit answer about his water and goes into this tirade about it. I stopped asking. Some people have to learn the hard way. He has no job, no money, and in my opinion no common sense. My parents are supporting his 45 year old a$$, soon to be 46.

* * *

Lesson: Know people triggers. High blood pressure is not to be played with; there is no cure but it can be maintained properly.

14

FUNNY TAMPA STORY

I told my friend, Stacy, I was going to write about this story.

Picture this: We drove from Orlando to Tampa to attend my childhood friends' wedding, Anthony.

Anthony was a dry-bragger. It often amazes me how some people feel that good about themselves and resort to bragging. I am not saying you shouldn't feel good about yourself, on the contrary, but bragging is annoying. To me it is a form of low self-esteem. Anthony had a very nice house and a luxury car, BMW. Anthony was from the "hood" as well and grew up poor like myself. One day Anthony, Stacy, and I went to the grocery store in his luxury car. Anthony starting bragging about the functions of his BMW; this was the first time he met Stacy and didn't know what to expect. He definitely didn't know SHE was not the one to brag in front of. He started giving voice commands to his car (dry-bragging); this was one of the luxury functions his BMW conveyed. He started telling the car to "play the CD". I guess it would not listen to his voice command and would not comply; so Stacy blurted out "two all-beef patties, special sauce, lettuce, cheese, pickles onions on a sesame seed bun; if you want to impress me, get me a burger out this mother-fucker". The laughter commenced and the insults flooded. Anthony said "Oh, you guys got jokes". Needless to say the dry bragging came to an end.

* * *

**Lesson: Know your audience.
Everybody is NOT enumerated by you
or your possessions.**

15

SOUTH STREET SEA-PORT

I was hanging out at the South Street Sea-Port with my two friends, Louie and Stacy. Louie also brought his then girlfriend, Darlene. Darlene, Stacy, and I also became friends through Louie. Darlene was one of the cool girl-friends of Louie that Stacy and I liked; the ones before her, not so much. We ordered some finger foods and were sitting at the table chopping it up and laughing. Darlene was telling us a story and she mentioned Louie having to clean his teeth and put them in a cup. I looked at her and said, "Did you say Louie put his teeth in a cup"? She said yes. I looked at Louie and asked him was he wearing dentures; is that true? I looked at Stacy and asked her did she know Louie had false teeth. She said, no. This was the first time we heard of such a thing. At this point we had been friends for almost ten years. I'll be damned! He hid this fact from us all this time. For some reason Stacy and I thought it was the funniest thing we ever heard. I can only guess it was a secret because he kept this little known fact from us and it took a girlfriend, he just met, to bring it out in the open. We commenced to making jokes, pretending WE didn't have any teeth. At this point Darlene and Louie didn't think our jokes were funny; but Stacy and I did! We laughed for what seemed like eternity, stomachs aching from laughter. On hindsight; were we hurting Louie's feelings by laughing? Am I wrong that it still makes me laugh to this day? I love you, Louie!

✳ ✳ ✳

Lesson: Some things are better left a secret. It may get into the wrong hands. Laughter is golden!

16

PHILLY

Some of my best times were spent in Philadelphia, Pennsylvania. My cousin Victor and I were thick as thieves once upon a time. I used to drive to Philly to hang out with Victor. Victor, in my opinion missed his calling; he should have been a stand-up comedian. Victor called me one weekend and said, "Let's hang out, cuz. I didn't have anything else to do this particular weekend and called my rode-dog, Stacy and asked her if she wanted to hang. Off we went. We started out at "Bahama Bay" (club on the pier) and hit about five additional clubs that night. The band was playing that night, I was the designated driver. Victor and Stacy took advantage of being passengers and par-took of the libations. We made a stop at Victor's then girlfriends' house. She (the girlfriend) wasn't happy about our visit. I'm sure she thought Stacy and I were Victor's women for the night. Victor is good looking and a playboy of sorts. The alleged jilted girlfriend commenced to throwing his belongings out the window. Clothes and Victor's underwear were landing in trees. Victor had to get a shopping bag and retrieve his things. That mishap didn't deter us from having FUN, it was a very entertaining way to start the fun filled evening! We made sure of that.

�֍ ֍ ֍

Lesson: Laughter is golden! You don't get to choose your family; life IS like a box of chocolates you never know what you are going to get.

17

HONESTY

It's time for an honest moment. It takes two to fuck up a marriage! I have to admit that my marriage was not all bad. We had some good times. I also have to admit to myself that I do still have a little bit of love for my soon to be ex-husband. He still needs therapy, very badly. He doesn't think so, but I KNOW so. Anytime you go from woman to woman to "kiss away the lonely'; you need to STOP and think about whom you are hurting in the large scheme of things. In the words of Forest Gump, "That's all I have to say about that".

I was sitting back listening to music; Jill Scott was playing (love her) "Just running across my mind"; reflecting. I think Jill Scott wrote that song for me. The lyrics brought me back to a past relationship. Every woman that I speak to have that one special someone in their past life that always will float into her mind. That doesn't mean you want to go back to them, it only means you might consider it, lol. I often wonder does that person feel the same way about me. I would like to think so, but that doesn't mean it is so. That has to be where hit songs come from, "life experiences". It is where my writings come from; it can't be different. My absolute favorite Prince song is, "Adore". Did Prince have an inspiration for this song? I would love to have a person feel that way about me and vice versa. Then again, that kind of feeling could be dangerous and I am definitely not in the market for that.

* * *

Lesson: It takes two. Treasure good relationships.

18

MORE
REFLECTIONS

Good friends are priceless. My good friend, Yves, is coming to my home to help me with some renovations. Yves is very good at home renovations and he loves doing them. I told him of some work that I needed done in and out of my home and he told me not to worry about it. He is going to come down from NYC and do this work for me. We have been friends for almost 30 years. Yves was a hang-out partner of mine. We used to club every weekend. I remember one time I invited my hair dresser Scottie along. I soon discovered homophobic attitudes some people have. Yves was not the homophobic person, his buddy was. It was myself, two of my friends, and two of Yves friends. When I think back, his friends must have viewed this hanging-out as a hookup situation. I did not. I thought we was going out partying to have a good time. Yves friend (I forgot his name) was homophobic. You know what they say about people that show that much animosity to a gay person, they themselves have gay tendencies. In other words, they are probably gay themselves or bi-sexual. My hair dresser, Scottie was a feminine gay person. Scottie had a lot of feminine energy and was proud. I loved Scottie and he was always fun to hang out with. That's the night I discovered you have to put your friends in groups. Weed smokers, holy rollers, people who don't give a damn either way (my favs), cigarette smokers, homosexuals, stuck-ups, etc.; the list goes on. The one group I did not mention was the ones who I don't care to fuck with; reason being. Damn this corona virus (Covid-19); has the whole country on lock down.

* * *

Lesson: 2 Timothy 3:1-17; But know this, that in the last days critical times hard to deal with will be here.

19

TODAY WAS A GOOD DAY

I realized that I don't give myself the credit I deserve. Case in point my ex, husband number two, called me today. He knows my good friend, Pearl, who was visiting when he called. He called me, "Bargain-Betty" and Pearl agreed with him and they laughed. It was at that moment I realized these were good traits of mine. I like good quality stuff, clothes, shoes, furniture, houses etc. These things don't have to be designer or high priced. As long as it looks good to me, it will do. However, I will only get these things on sale. I never pay full price. It doesn't have to be "in season" I can wait for next season. I like to think I have an eye for fashion. At least that's what others have told me. I'm starting to believe them or I'm just that confident. I have some items that are 25 years old that still look good and are fashionable; but fashion only changes slightly. It repeats itself in circle formation.

I don't give myself enough credit. My daughter once said to me, "She always thought her mom was fierce". That floored me. I didn't think my daughter thought that of me. My sister-cousin once said, "You always look like you stepped out the pages of Essence magazine. I thought to myself, "Girl you must be doing something right". It is time I start thinking about myself in that manner. Maybe I will stop attracting scrubs. Actually, I have to stop accepting scrubs in my life.

✻ ✻ ✻

Lesson: I am the bomb.com.

20

JUST THINKING...

I was getting dressed and got into my "feelings", and thought had I stayed with husband number three, I would be one of those bitches I talk about. You know the one that stayed with a man who was clearly cheating on her. It occurred to me that I truly didn't know how to pick a man. It's one thing to pick the wrong man, but it's another thing to know this and marry him anyway. That's some stupid shit. That is why I am convinced that it takes two to fuck up a marriage. I'm putting this shit in writing, "I WILL NOT EVER GET MARRIED AGAIN". That is what I want put in my obituary. Those who knew me know that to be true. She died, single.

* * *

Lesson: It takes two. Go with your gut feeling.

21

DISABILITY

Am I disabled? Fuck yeah! I cannot sit here and feel sorry for myself, but I can FIGHT for what is rightfully mine. I did not ask to get this disease. Lord knows I fight to prevent this disease from taking over me. Sometimes I feel God is punishing me for all the wrong I did in my life. I strongly believe you reap what you sew. Hell, I'm reaping. I sometimes tell myself, I have MS, MS doesn't have me. That's some bullshit. Sometimes, this shit has me. I have to admit, having a positive attitude does a world of good. Lately, I have been feeling more trusting in Jehovah. He has pulled me through some tough shit. I feel bad when I curse and mention God in the next sentence; however a curse word sometimes says it better.

My good friend, Pearl, drops wisdom on me that I need at the right time. She has a way of making you always see the blessings that God saw you through. The government keeps denying my disability. Shit, I'm, disabled! The government wants you to be on your death bed before they grant you what is rightfully yours. I've been working since I was fifteen years old, I'm fifty three now. I just did the math and that amounts to thirty nine years of my paying into FICA. Now I need it, so be it. I guess I am paying for the mother-fuckers that NEVER paid FICA.

❋ ❋ ❋

Lesson: Trust in God, he will not forsake you. Life isn't always fair as you like. You reap what you sew. All that glitters isn't gold.

22

THE WOMAN IN
THE MIRROR

My girlfriend told me to take a look at myself in the mirror and take accountability of the person I see. I received
divorce papers in the mail directly from husband number three. The papers seem to have been conjured up
through "Rocket Lawyer". I scanned them and sent them
to my lawyer. He emailed me back and said, "DO NOT
sign anything"! That's all I needed to hear. I can only spec-
ulate as to why these papers did not come through his
lawyer. My speculations may or may not be wrong, but I
have to ask myself why I care. I don't want to lose. If I lose
anything I have, to me, it shows weakness. I always want
to be considered a "strong black woman". Sometimes I
feel like a weakling. I delve in self-pity at times. Why do I
feel the need to know "Why"? What can I do if I KNEW?

Nothing; not a damn thing. Other times I feel like I can concur the world and I charge into motion. Then something brings me back down to reality. The reality is, I'm broke and can't pay attention. I have to think and grow rich as my coach J would say. That means I have to think of ways I can make money massively. I do have a plan in my head of how I will get started. I only repeat it to myself because I don't want anybody telling me it's not a good plan. I am of the "show me" crew; when I should have seeped out my elders' advice.

❊ ❊ ❊

Lesson: Move on! The person in the mirror is the main one YOU have to count on.

23

URPRISE!

Urprise is what my nephew used to say when he was a toddler because he couldn't pronounce the word surprise. My ex-boyfriend contacted me out of the blue. I haven't spoken to him since 2013. He exaggerated the time lapse and said it's been 20 years. I guess 7 years seemed like 20 to him. You never know when two people paths will cross again. At first I felt pleasantly surprised by his call until he told me he had a live-in girlfriend for the past six or seven years. That flattered feeling turned into pisstivity. Living with someone is a marriage all day long if you ask me. You may not be legally married but commitment is commitment. That reminded me of why this individual was an ex. He didn't believe in marriage and vowed to be a bachelor the rest of his life. I don't believe in marriage either, but at least I can say that I tried it at least once. In my case three times, but not anymore. Although I was flattered to know that he was thinking of me (we did have some good times), my right mind tells me, "don't fuck with him", and so I won't. It's amazing to me that people resort back to what's familiar to them, but I remember what we used to do; that's the shit that has me stuck. When I do some further exploring into my psyche, I'm really not fuckin with this n^&&@ no more. My mental sanity has become more important to me than a good roll in the hay. My girlfriend said to me "Life went on for him; you're the one that's stuck. Ok, I get it.

❖ ❖ ❖

Lesson: Leave the past in the past.
People are exes for a reason.

24

KNOWING YOURSELF

Today I learned something about myself. I don't think my self-worth was nurtured growing up. My dad never said nice things about me or to me. If he was proud of me, I never knew. If he thought I was beautiful, I never knew. If he thought I was smart. I never knew. I wonder what he thinks of me today. I may never know. What I do know is he loves me.

Right now I am pissed. What do you do when someone talks behind your back? They said you were lazy and need to get up off your ass and do something. This is a person who got evicted from her home and her car re-possessed. How fuckin dare you? Why? I am offended. I think I'd rather live alone. I was getting used to it and loving it.

* * *

Lesson: Live your best life, YOLO!

25

FRIEND ZONE

It has occurred to me that some men do not know when they will forever be in the "friend zone". I have a friend that has a lot of confidence in himself. He does not know when he has been placed in the "friend zone". I just had a conversation with this friend and came from the conversation feeling that this guy is creepy. Then I thought, I need to pull away from this person because even though he says creepy things, he's harmless but there is nothing about this guy I am remotely attracted to. I really need to stay single for the next ten years. Single means dating as well. That's all folks.

✳ ✳ ✳

Lesson: Friends come in all facades

26

I JUST REMEMBERED....

This is how I found out husband number 2 was cheating on me. I was at work and my husband called me on his cell phone as he usually does; another call came through for him and he put me on hold. I was at work and I had to free up my phone line so I hung up the phone. A few seconds later the phone rings and before I can say a word I heard voices on the line. It was husband no. 2 and his friend talking about how husband no. 2's mistress, Gwen, is threatening to tell me, the wife, all about the affair. I butted in and said, "I heard enough, how could you. Crickets. I hung up the phone.

* * *

Lesson: When you're on your cell phone and another call comes through, end your current call be before you answer an incoming call.

27

SINGLE AGAIN

I was just served with divorce papers (May 21, 2020)! The sheriff came to my door and frightened me. My first thought was something happened to one of my sons. They are both in the military and I immediately thought the worse. Thankfully it was just divorce papers. I faxed them over to my attorney and he said I didn't have to do anything. I then felt a sense of relief; almost as if an albatross had been lifted. I am soon to be single again and I feel grateful and free. My final divorce papers came a day after on my birthday. Yeah!!

✤ ✤ ✤

Lesson: Do not jump to conclusions until you know the facts.

ABOUT THE
AUTHOR

Audra was born and raised in Brooklyn, NY. She has three adult children and three grandchildren and resides in Concord, NC.

CPSIA information can be obtained
at www.ICGtesting.com
Printed in the USA
LVHW021510010921
696662LV00015B/1136

9 781649 904201